STREAKS OF SHORT STORIES

INTELLECTS OF TINY BUDS

S. SUMATHI

DEDICATION

I solely dedicate this "STREAKS OF SHORT STORIES"

- To all short story lovers,
- To all language lovers,
- To all my students who had contributed to this book and those who hadn't contributed to this book.
- To my family and friends.
- To my consort and ward without whom I'm zero.

Contents

Contents

Prologue

STREAKS OF SHORT STORIES

(INTELLECTS OF TINY BUDS)

AN ANTHOLOGY OF SHORT STORIES BY TNSB STUDENTS

EDITOR & COMPILER
MRS. S. SUMATHI,
M.A., B.Ed.,

Disclaimer

This short story book "STREAKS OF SHORT STORIES", is completely a work of fiction. The characters, places, events or incidents mentioned here are fictitious and some may be the own experience of the co-authors. Any resemblance to actual persons or actual events is purely coincidental.

Editor & Compiler
Mrs. S. Sumathi

Disclaimer

This [illegible] work of fiction. [illegible] characters [illegible] and incidents mentioned here are fictitious and [illegible] the [illegible]. Any resemblance [illegible] purely coincidental.

[illegible]

[illegible]

Preface

EDITOR'S VOICE

"Literacy is the bridge
To move from misery to hope.
Books are the steps in that bridge."

Books help us fight off ignorance. Reading makes our brain alive. They are the finest mind freshner. They are the package of knowledge. They are the undemanding faithful friends that never walks away from us. Books are the worthy best gift and a tool to sharp our intellect. To sharp the intellect, here is the "STREAKS OF SHORT STORIES", the intellects of tiny buds of the Tamil Nadu state board students.

This anthology contains thirty short stories written by TNSB students of class 9. Each story will be a special feast to the all who love reading short stories. It is just a try to inspire and to encourage the children to present their ideas and thoughts, their own experience or the events happened around them as a story. The editor is sure that those who read the book will enjoy a lot. The editor promises that this book will be the sweetest treat for the short story lovers.

Mrs. S. Sumathi, M.A., B.Ed.,
Editor & Compiler.

Acknowledgements

"Always have an attitude of gratitude."

Sterling K. Brown

A grateful heart always seems as a graceful heart. As a graceful heart, I just want to express my deep gratitude to my consort and my little princess for their non-stop support. Words can't express how much they mean to me.

Hereby I'm sending a heartfelt thanks to Mrs. D. Brinda, Teacher, GHS, Melpattampakkam, Cuddalore dt, who held my hands and started my writing journey.

I'm eternally grateful to Mr. K. Sankar, Headmaster, Sri KGS Hr. Sec. School, Aduthurai, Tanjore dt., and Mr. K. Selvam, Assistant Headmaster, Sri KGS Hr. Sec. School, Aduthurai, Tanjore dt, for their continuous and complete support in publishing the book by encouraging the students and for sparing their precious time to render a wonderful foreword.

I would like to extend my deepest gratitude to Mr. G. Thiraviyakumar, Teacher, GBHSS, Pandanallur, Tanjore dt, who is always ready to lend a helping hand in editing the content. I'd like to extend my thanks from the depth of my heart to Mrs. Y. Princillin Joan, Mrs. Anshi Pratiba Daugh, Mrs.S. Yamini Priya, Mrs. T. Jayalakshmi and Mrs. G. Geetha for spending their valuable time inspite of their busy schedule for editing the stories.

I would like to pay my special regards to the co-authors, the tiny budding writers of the book because the project wouldn't have been possible without them.

Thank you one and all who helps me in making this book to publish as a paperback successfully.

Foreword

Mr. K. Sankar, Msc., B.Ed., M.Phil, PGDCAHeadmasterSri KGS Hr Sec School,Aduthurai

Mrs. S. Sumathi, M.A.(ENG), B.Ed., is serving in Sri KGS Higher Secondary School, Aduthurai, as a Graduate English Teacher. She is known for her dedication and selfless service to student community. As an author, she has published two books of 100 poems each namely "String of Pearls" and "Drizzling of Verses." She has co-authored some books of poetry and two books of short stories. She is a receiver of many awards. She proves to be a committed and responsible person in executing all sort of academics related works. She wishes to be a great teacher and the best human. I wish her a great success in all steps of her life.

As a special initiative, she made the students of class 9 to write short stories. As an inspirer, she inspired the students to

write stories. She then edited it and as a result here comes "Streaks of short stories", the intellects of tiny buds. It is really an amazing work. The style of writing is easy to understand. The language used is simple and relevant too. Each and every story is excellent indicating the meaning of life. I wish the co-authors of the book to write more and more and achieve more and more in their life. From the depth of my heart, I wish them all a bright future.

(K. SANKAR)

Foreword

Mr. M. Selvam, M.Sc., B.Ed., M.Phil,Assistant Headmaster,Sri KGS Hr. Sec. School,Aduthurai.

I'm indeed very elated to write a foreword for this book "Streaks of short stories." I'm happy to mention about S. Vaishnavi of class 9. She wrote about "An ambitious girl" and how she developed from rag to rich position. The story deals how a girl worked hard and became a successful business woman. She presented the story in a beautiful manner and I am sure that it will motivate a lot of unemployed persons. I really congratulate her for her unique way of thinking.

I would like to convey my happiness to write about M. Akshaya of class 9. "Self-confidence" a story that mentions about the struggles a girl faced to get a doctoral degree in medicine. Her imagination is indeed very brilliant. In future she may write more stories for children.

I felt contented to mention about the story "Lovely friendship", written by M. Bhuvaneshwaran of class 9. His love and care for animals was expressed well through the story in an excellent manner. He paved a way for the children to have love and care for animals.

I am proud to say that Mrs. S. Sumathi, an English graduate teacher has been working in Sri KGS Hr. Sec. school since 2012. She is the editor and publisher of this excellent collection of short stories. She has already published two books of poem collection written by her namely "String of Pearls" and "Drizzling of Verses." Most of her poems speak about traditional beliefs. In my point of view, I believe that Mrs. S. Sumathi is making a good society. I would like to convey my best wishes for her future endeavour too.

(M. SELVAM)

CHAPTER ONE

COMPASSION

R. ABINAYA,CLASS 9, Sri KGS HSS, Aduthurai.

Once there was a man named Shankar in a village. He belonged to a poor family. He was a single man. He was a wood cutter. He sold woods to run his life. One day, he was walking through the forest carrying some woods on his head. On the way, he saw an old man. He was very hungry. He looked very feeble and tired. He begged Shankar for some food. Immediately Shankar gave the food he bought for him without keeping anything for him as he was a man of compassion. Then he started moving ahead again.

After walking few minutes, he saw a deer lying down very tired. It couldn't walk even a single step as it felt very thirsty and yearned for water. Shankar understood this and helped the deer by giving water to it. The deer was alright after drinking enough water. The deer looked at him thankfully and licked him with love. Shankar felt happy and satisfied on seeing this. He started walking again on his way.

Few minutes later, on his way he saw an old lady shivering in cold. She tried to ignite fire. But she failed as she didn't have enough woods and fire. Shankar saw this and helped the lady with his woods to camp a fire. Once the lady started feeling well, Shankar left the place happily. Already it grew dark. His hut was near the forest. He walked fast to reach his hut. Unfortunately, he was bitten by a snake. It hurts him badly. The deer that was helped by Shankar saw this. It went to the old lady for help. They arrived at the place where Shankar fainted with the guidance of the deer. They both treated Shankar well with the available herbs. Slowly Shankar got relieved and felt alright. All were happy that they were able to help other.

LET OUR HEARTS BE STRETCHED OUT IN COMPASSION FOR EVERYONE.

CHAPTER TWO

SELF-CONFIDENCE

M. AKSHAYA,CLASS 9, Sri KGS HSS, Aduthurai

One beautiful and lovable family lived in a village. Akshaya was the princess of the family. She lived happily with her parents and grandparents. Unfortunately, Akshaya lost her mother. She died due to lack of hospital facilities in her village. So Akshaya determined to become a doctor and wished to serve and save her village and her people. She decided to go to a metro city to make her dream come true. But her father didn't permit her as he couldn't afford the fee for her education due to poverty. Akshaya was greatly disappointed but she was very strong in her aim. With the complete support of her grandmother, Akshaya went to a city. First, she searched and find a suitable part time job for her. Then she joined a medical college with fee concession because of her knowledge and talent. Though she faced many struggles, obstacles and problems, she successfully completed her studies with her grandma's blessings and encouragement. She returned to her village as the best doctor. Yet her father was angry with her. She started practicing as a doctor and served her people whole heartedly. Everyone in the village appreciated her and loved her very much because of her selfless service. She wished to meet her grandmother but her father didn't allow her to meet. Suddenly, one day, her grandma felt ill seriously. The time was eleven at night. Grandma struggled to breathe. When Akshaya came to know this, she rushed to save her grandma. She treated her well. Grandma's life was saved. Akshaya's father realized his mistake. Now he appreciated his daughter's confidence and courage. He felt very proud of his daughter.

SELF CONFIDENCE, THE SUPER POWER IS ESSENTIAL FOR EVERY HUMAN.

CHAPTER THREE

TIME CHANGES EVERYTHING

A. AGASTIN,CLASS 9, Sri KGS HSS, Aduthurai

A farmer named Charles lived in a village. He lived with his wife Mary and with his daughter Jhansi. Jhansi was in her grade 5. Her ambition was to become an IAS Officer by clearing the UPSC examinations. Charles was a good hardworking farmer. To improve his income, he decided to do vegetables and fruit farming in his lands that is chemical free. He approached a bank for loan to make his life better by farming. At that time, the local landlord of the village seized his lands as he borrowed some money from him already. It was a great shock to Charles. He was completely broken. He became blank. He didn't know what to do, how to handle the situation and how to overcome it. He felt in depression. He started drinking alcohol to forget the bad happenings of his life. Every day he drank alcohol, came home and beat his wife. It became a regular activity. One day when he came and beat his wife, it ended in a big fight. Charles slept well after the fight. Next morning, when he woke up, there was a crowd in his house. He went near to see what had happened. He was shocked to hear that his wife committed suicide and died. His daughter was crying. Charles stood still as a statue. Later Mary's dead body was taken to the graveyard. Charles wasn't ready to move to the graveyard. He felt guilty that he was the reason for his wife's death. But he didn't stop drinking alcohol. He stopped going to the church. One day when he crossed the church, he heard the prayer of his daughter. She prayed that she too wanted to die as her father was still a drunkard and he was not taking care of her. Charles realized his mistake and stopped drinking. He filed a case against the landlord, won the case and got back his lands. Once again happily he started his farming. He worked hard and earned good profit. Little by little he improved a lot in his farming and became a successful man. Jhansi also studied well. She worked hard to make her dream come true. She too achieved his ambition. Charles understood that "Everything changes with time."

TIME HEALS EVERYTHING.

CHAPTER FOUR

EDUCATION, THE BEST WEAPON

R. ARCHANA,CLASS 9, Sri KGS HSS, Aduthurai

In a village, there lived a happy family though they were poor. The father's name was Ramu, the mother's name was Mallika and their only daughter was Roja. Ramu was a farmer and he worked as a labour in a landlord's house. Mallika was a house wife. Roja was studying class eight. Life went well. They were satisfied with what they had and lived happily with what they got. Suddenly Ramu felt seriously ill. They went to the hospital. Doctors after examining him, they advised for many tests. Then they confirmed that Ramu was affected by blood cancer. They also added that he couldn't be cured as his illness was chronic. Anyway, the doctors tried their level best to save Ramu. Yet he died. Mallika and Roja were left alone. None of their relatives helped them. Mallika advised Roja a lot to study well as education is the only way to make our life better. She motivated Roja to study well to get a good job and to stand on her own. Mallika faced many hardships to raise Roja but she did it happily for her daughter's sake. Roja too understood her mother's love and the hardships she was facing for her sake. Roja too studied well and shone bright. To her bad luck, Mallika felt ill. Roja tried a lot to save her mother. Mallika was in her death bed. At that time too, Mallika told Roja never to trust anyone and advised her always to be good and to do good to everyone. She also insisted Roja to help the poor and the needy with whatever was possible for her. Mallika's soul went to deep slumber while uttering these words to Roja. Roja felt so sad. She thought her parents as her god, studied well as per her mother's advise and settled in a good position. She started doing everything as per her mother's last wish. She lived boldly and happily. Though everyone left her alone, her boldness and education only supported her and raised her status. She lived happily doing good to others.

EDUCATION IS THE PASSPORT TO FUTURE.

CHAPTER FIVE

BEING GOOD

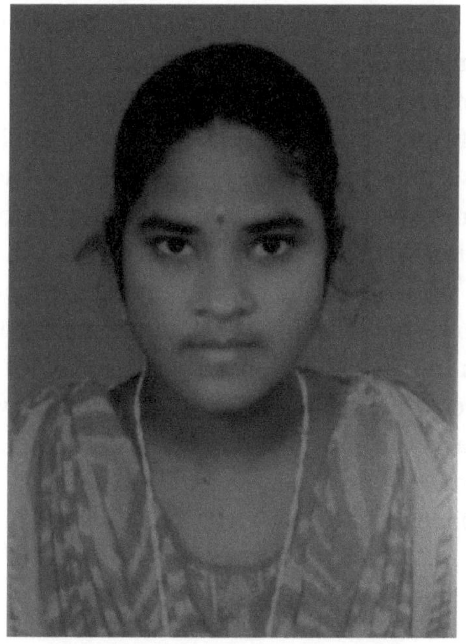

R. ATCHAYA,CLASS 9, Sri KGS HSS, Aduthurai

Swaminathan lived in a town. He was a hardworking farmer who had a garden on his own. He plucked flowers from his garden and sold them at the market regularly. But the income was insufficient to run his family as his business was not so good though he worked hard. There was a temple on the way to his home. After completing his business, he used to go to the temple every day. That day also he went to the temple, prayed well and sat in the temple. He looked very sad. The priest of the temple knew Swaminathan very well as he visited the temple regularly. The priest asked the reason for Swaminathan's sadness. He told about the loss in business and the distress in his family. The priest consoled him that everything will be alright soon. After having some healthy discussion, he left home. He saw a box on the way to home. He took it, opened and shocked to see the lump sum money. He searched whether anyone is looking for the money. An old man was searching for the money with a worried face. Swami approached him and handed over the money to him. The old man was very happy. He thanked Swami and blessed him for his honesty. Swami was very happy too.

He moved from there to home. On the way, an old lady begged for food. She seemed very feeble. Though Swami had only a small amount of money with him, he decided to get food for the old lady. He did the same what he thought. The old lady happily blessed Swami. Swami started walking home thinking a lot about improving his business and increasing his income. Suddenly God appeared before him and said that he only came as the old man and the old lady to check him. The Almighty blessed him with abundant health and wealth for his kind and good nature. Swami's life began to prosper because of his kindness and loyalty.

BE GOOD, DO GOOD, GOOD THINGS WILL FALL IN A LINE.

CHAPTER SIX

THE HORROR HOUSE

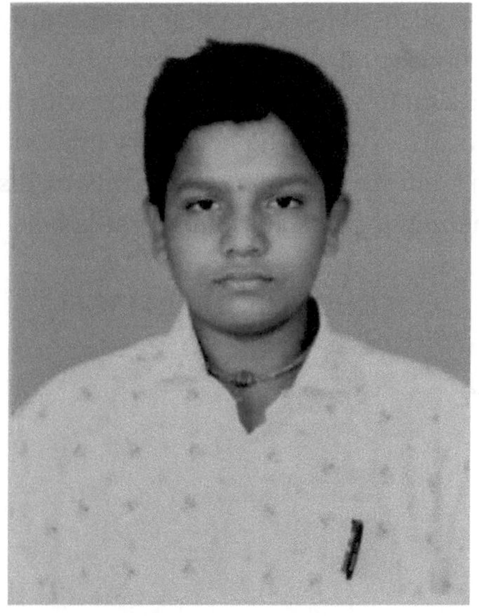

K. BALAJI,CLASS 9, Sri KGS HSS, Aduthurai

Once upon a time there was a boy named Kavin. He was studying in class seven at Government high school, Siva Gangai. After his school hours, he and his friends used to play in their school playground regularly. That day also they were playing. It grew darker. The watch man came and insisted the boys to leave the ground. Kavin and his friends went home. When Kavin reached his house, his mother welcomed him and enquired why he was late. Then she told him to refresh himself. When Kavin came back after refreshing, his mother requested him to go to a grocery shop to buy some necessary groceries. Kavin also left to the shop. On the way he saw a scary house. When he was crossing the house, he heard some scary noises inside the house. The street dog too barked loudly. Out of curiosity, Kavin entered the gate. He looked here and there inside the gate. Suddenly a voice ordered him to get into the house. Though he was afraid a little, he managed to get into the house. He saw a ghost there. Kavin started speaking to it and asked about it. The ghost replied that it was Ravi and the scary house was theirs. The ghost also added that their total family died in a fire accident in the house and it told the whole story of their family. It also requested Kavin to visit it often and play with it. Kavin assured and left the place. He bought the necessary groceries and returned home. He didn't inform anything about this to his mother as he thought that she might be afraid. But Kavin is bold enough to face the ghost.

GHOSTLY GREETINGS!

CHAPTER SEVEN

LOVELY FRIENDSHIP

M. BHUVANESHWARAN,CLASS 9, Sri KGS HSS, Aduthurai

Once there lived two gorillas in a forest. They were very thick and close friends. Both lived happily in the forest. They spent their morning time in finding food. During afternoon, they would rest on one of their favorite trees in the forest. Then they would sleep in their caves in the forest at night. One evening, a team of four hunters entered the forest. They searched for animals for a very long time but they didn't get anything. As it was too late and felt too tired, they looked for a better place to camp in the forest. They saw a pond in a place. They decided to camp near the pond. They made a tent and camped near the pond. After sometime one of the gorillas came out of the cave to drink water in the pond. After drinking water, it ate some fruits. Then it climbed up a tree to rest. The hunters team looked at the gorilla and followed it. When it sat on the tree, they silently went near the gorilla and caught it. They tied it and kept it in an iron cage. Then they closed the cage completely with a sheet and moved to the camp. They had some fruits and sandwiches. They listened and enjoyed music for a while. Then everyone slept due to tiredness. The other gorilla woke up and searched its friend. It searched in all their favorite places usually where they both used to go. But it couldn't find his friend. Without giving hope, it wandered here and there in search of its friend. It went near the pond. It noticed the huge thing covered with the sheet. It slowly went near the cage and sniffed. Then removed the sheet and found his friend. It also looked at the camp. The hunters were all in deep sleep. Suddenly it ran for help to save his friend. It brough the king of the forest and the elephant for help. The lion roared loudly. The hunters got panicked and they all ran away. Then with the help of the lion and the elephant, the gorilla saved its friend. All the animals went happily. The friendship of the two gorillas lasted forever.

TRUE FRIENDS ARE NEVER APART.

CHAPTER EIGHT

THE TURNING POINT

S.B. DHARANI,CLASS 9, Sri KGS HSS, Aduthurai

Ezhil's family was a small family who lived in the out skirts of Chennai. She lived with her parents and her brother Kumar. Ezhil was eleven years and Kumar was nine years old. Ezhil loved playing kabaddi and was very talented in it. She participated in many school level competitions and won many matches. Though they were poor, they lived happily with what they had. Here came the struggle and a great loss for their family. Ezhil's father expired in a road accident. Ezhil's life turned upside down. Her mother went to work in some houses and offices for their livelihood. Ezhil had to stop her education to take care of her brother and the household chores. Sometimes Ezhil went with her mother to the house where she worked. While she went there, she used to play Kabaddi with the children of their master. The master noticed her wonderful sportsmanship. Actually, he was a retired Kabaddi team coach. He started coaching Ezhil. Ezhil improved a lot in her play day by day. She was getting ready to take part in a national level match. Here came the struggle again in her life. She fell down and her left leg was badly fractured. She underwent an operation. But she didn't give up her hope. After a month, she started walking slowly and her practice also. She got well in due time. She participated in the National level match and won the game. She made her mother and her master proud. This became a great turning point in her life.

OPPORTUNITY KNOCKS THE DOOR ONCE, NEVER GO BEHIND REASONS.

CHAPTER NINE

HARDWORK

V.DHARANI,CLASS 9, Sri KGS HSS, Aduthurai

A poor couple lived in a village. The husband's name was Ram and the wife's name was Radha. They were poor so that they ate only once in a day. They didn't know what to do and how to improve their life style. They thought no one should suffer due to starvation and thought of doing something for that. When they both were talking, they heard a loud noise and the loud screaming of a lady. Ram and Radha went out to see what had happened. They saw a car that crashed into a tree. Inside the car, there was a lady sitting. The lady was wounded and moaning in pain. Radha helped her to get out of the car and took her to her house. She gave her water to drink. The lady requested Ram to help her and pleaded him to do a favor for her. She handed over a briefcase of money and told Ram to hand over the same to a rich man in the nearby town. Without any hesitation, Ram did what the lady said to him very honestly. The rich man of the nearby town praised Ram for his honesty and gave him some money as a reward. He returned to his home and informed the lady what had happened. The lady too was too happy with Ram and Radha for their timely help. She enquired about their job and their income. They told everything about the difficulties and struggles of their life. Suddenly the lady gave them some money to start a business as an honor for their honesty and helping tendency. With the money received, they started a road side hotel. They both worked hard day and night. They provided tasty food. Their business improved a lot. Whoever came hungry to them, they provided them food for free of cost as they didn't want anyone to suffer from starvation. They earned a lot and opened a new restaurant. Their business went well. They built a new house and lived happily ever after.

HARDWORK WILL ALWAYS EARN SUCCESS.

CHAPTER TEN

MYSTERY OF LOVE

R. DHARANEESHWARI,CLASS 9, Sri KGS HSS, Aduthurai

Janaki and her son lived in a lonely house. Her husband died in an accident. So, Janaki went to some houses as a servant maid to get their basic needs. Always she used to wear torn sarees. They suffered a lot even to have their food at least twice a day. But even in this toughest situation too, Janaki never failed to send her son to school. Her son's name was Raj. He was a very tenderhearted boy with a kind and helpful mind. One day his teacher informed all the students that the school was going to celebrate "Mother's Day." Raj thought of getting a nice and lovable gift for his mother. He got confused what to get for her. Finally, he decided to buy a beautiful saree as he knew very well that his mother never had a good saree. But he had no money to get a saree. So, he was determined to earn the necessary money by going to a job. He went to a departmental store near his school and asked for a job. The owner of the shop enquired why he was coming for the job. Raj told everything to the owner. The owner of the shop understood Raj's kindness and love for his mother and was very happy about his intention for coming to the job. He told Raj to come to his shop after his school hours. After completing his classes, Raj worked in the shop and he would reach the home before his mother's arrival. It continued everyday till he earned a good amount of money to get the saree. Once he got the money needed, he bought a beautiful saree for his mother happily. On his way back to home, a car passed him splashing dirty water. He started weeping. The owner of the car apologized and gave him some money. Raj bought some sweets and food with that. He started walking home. On the way, he met a mother and his son. They looked very tired and hungry. Raj gave the food to them. He felt happy when he witnessed their happy faces. He reached home with the sweets alone but with complete satisfaction. To his surprise, Raj's mother was wearing a new saree. She hugged Raj with love, care and affection. Raj wished her mother for Mother's Day by giving the sweets to her. It was a mystery for Raj how his mother got the new saree.

THE ONLY THING WE NEVER GET ENOUGH IS LOVE.

CHAPTER ELEVEN

FAILURES ARE STEPPING STONE

B. DHIYA,CLASS 9, Sri KGS HSS, Aduthurai.

Kavitha was a cute little girl. She lived in a village with her family. Her family was a small family. She lived happily with her father Suresh and her mother Mala. Their family was a poor family. Suresh wasn't educated well. So, he wished to make her daughter a graduate. But Kavitha was interested more in games than studies. She went to school only because of her father's wish and the other important thing to meet her physical education teacher. Kavitha played shotput very well. Her ambition was to take part in the Olympics. So, she came school regularly to learn more about the game from her Physical Education Teacher. She did all this without the knowledge of her father as he never liked Kavitha playing games. Kavitha hid everything from her father. One day, the school conducted parent teachers meeting. When Suresh came for the meeting, he came to know everything about Kavitha's interest in playing Shotput. Kavitha's PT teacher told Suresh that she was playing very well and one day she would become the pride of our place. Mala felt happy when she heard this but Suresh became too angry. He scolded Kavitha for not studying properly. Kavitha was so upset by her father's behavior. By this time, she went for a competition in shotput throw. Keeping the words of her father in mind, she lost the game. Kavitha's mother and her teacher motivated and encouraged her. Her teacher advised her to practice well with confidence and faith. Kavitha changed her attitude and started practicing well. After that she won many games. Little by little she corrected all her mistakes. Now she was ready for the Olympics with full energy and enthusiasm. She felt sure that she would succeed. Her father too after witnessing her success, never scolded her for playing.

LEARN FROM FAILURES
START A NEW PROCESS.

CHAPTER TWELVE

THE MAGICAL FRIEND

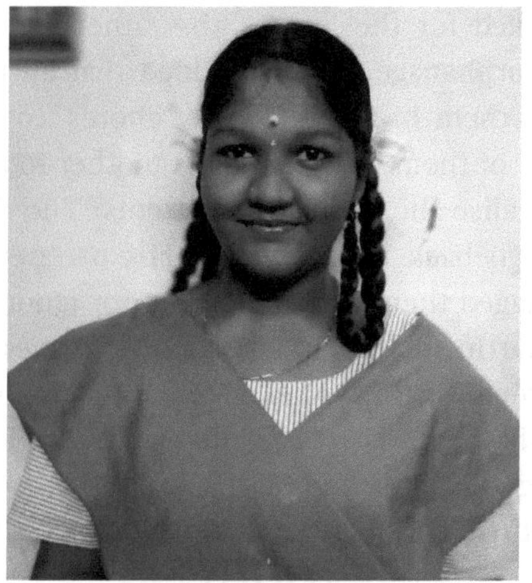

M. DURGA,CLASS 9, Sri KGS HSS, Aduthurai.

There was a new planet named Leiearth. People of the planet had many magical powers. They taught about magic in schools too. They had a special magic jacket. There was a teenage boy named Martin. He never gave respect to his parents. So, his parents thought of sending Martin to the earth for forty days to teach him a lesson. Martin reached earth. He saw not only the beauty of the earth but also the dangerous face of the earth. When he saw the children on earth, he thought that they were the lovable creation he had ever seen as they were the pure souls. Martin saw a group of children playing. They were funny and played happily near the river bank. Martin too joined them. There were two seven-year-old kids named Suseedran and Geetha, a ten-year-old girl named Varsha and two teenagers named Sumithran and Karthi. He spent his remaining days with them. Martin showed magic to his friends. One day he asked his friends to tell their wishes and also told that he would fulfill it. The two seven-year-old kids without any big dreams asked for a house full of chocolates. Varsha wished to have magical wings as she liked to go beyond the world. Sumithran asked for a magical speaking dog as he wished to know about the mind of the pets. Karthi sadly asked for the love of the father and the mother as he grew in an orphanage. He also added that all my friends had mother to help them in all their daily chores, to show true love and to take care of them. So, he asked a mother to beget love. This made Martin realise the love of his parents. The day came when Martin had to go back to his planet. His parents came to meet him. Martin hugged them and apologized for ignoring them. They were happy. Martin told about his friend's wishes. They fulfilled everything except Karthi's. Martin requested his parents to take Karthi too with them. They accepted and all went to Leiearth. Finally, Karthi got a family and Martin learnt a lesson.

NEVER IGNORE LOVE, IT WILL MAKE US REGRET ONEDAY.

CHAPTER THIRTEEN

BEING GRATEFUL

S. HARINI,CLASS 9, Sri KGS HSS, Aduthurai

Kamala was a widower. She lived in a town with her only daughter Varshini. Kamala worked in a rich man's house as a servant maid. Kamala and Varshini stayed in the outhouse of their master Mr. Rajan as they had no one. Varshini was a good-natured girl who was ready to help others always. She was smart and intelligent too. Rajan was a man of honesty, loyalty and generosity with helping tendency. He had only one son. Day rolled on normally. One day Kamala felt ill. She was diagnosed as brain tumour. At that time Varshini was also getting ready for her tenth common examination. She couldn't concentrate in her studies. She thought of her mother's bad condition always and worried a lot. By this time, Rajan came to help her. He advised Varshini to concentrate well in her studies. He also told her to try hard to get good marks in the examination as it was her mother's wish. He also added that he would take care of her mother. Varshini too followed his advice and scored very good marks. Unfortunately, Kamala expired. Rajan consoled Varshini. He helped and supported her a lot to continue her studies. Rajan's son also studied well but he was always jealous of Varshini as his father showed more love to her. Varshini and Rajan's son were grown up now. Rajan arranged a marriage to his son. His son and daughter-in-law were very happy. But they both hated Varshini. Because of their hatred, there was misunderstanding and fight at their home. Rajan's son and his wife were afraid that Rajan would write either half or full of his property to Varshini. The resentment continued to grow. When Varshini came to know all about this, she felt very sorry as she was the reason behind all these crises. She decided to leave the house. She informed Rajan and left the house. She completed her graduation and got a good job too. She settled in her life and lived happily with the true love of her master Rajan. Always she was thankful to Rajan.

BE THANKFUL TO GOD FOR WHAT WE HAVE.

CHAPTER FOURTEEN

DILIGENCE

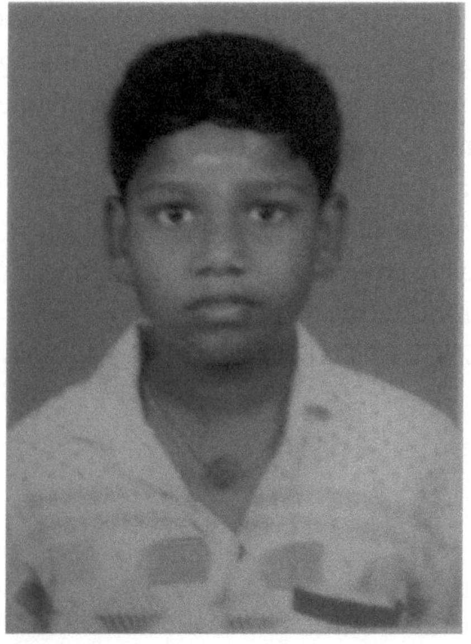

B. HARI SANKAR,CLASS 9, Sri KGS HSS, Aduthurai

A poor girl named Karpagam, sixteen years old lived in a village. The girl's father had no work. Her mother worked in some houses. She did the work of cleaning the utensils. Days rolled on. The girl's father expired. However, her mother managed to get married her daughter. Karpagam's husband was a milkman. She also worked in a tea shop for a meagre salary. Life was somewhat better for her. She gave birth to a male baby. Karpagam's husband died when her son was at the age of three. Her life turned upside down. The boy was so mischievous. She couldn't send him to school. At the age of eight, the boy too started working in a cycle shop. At the age of eleven, he started working in a hotel for a scanty salary. Then the village president gave him a good job. The girl's life began to improve a little because of his son's job. Some people of the village called the boy for financing work. But he refused strongly. He thought of doing catering as he was an expert in cooking. So, he started his business as a partner with a catering owner. Later, he left the catering owner due to his egoistic behavior. He decided to start his own catering service by the name of his mother Karpagam. He labored diligently round the clock. His cooking style and taste attracted everyone. He opened a hotel in the name "Sri Karpagam Vilas". He became rich and he got married. His marriage function was in a very grand manner. He invited many VIPs for the function especially the village president as the chief guest who supported him when he was in trouble and difficulty. He was very well settled in life because of his hard work.

DILIGENCE IS THE KEY TO UNIVERSAL SUCCESS.

CHAPTER FIFTEEN

A POOR FARMER

S. LATHA,CLASS 9, Sri KGS HSS, Aduthurai

A poor family lived in a village. The family had five persons. Ramu, the father, Raji, the mother lived with their two daughters and a son. All the three children were studying in a school. Ramu completed his schooling and he knew very well about the importance of education. So, he sent all his three children to school.

Ramu had a small land of his own and did farming in that to manage the household expenses and his children's educational expenses. Everyone in the family worked hard. Once when Ramu was waiting for the proper time to harvest his field, it rained heavily. All his crops drowned in water. It was a heavy loss for him. He didn't know how to manage the situation and how to overcome the hard situation. Ramu thought for a while and came to a conclusion. He decided to stop her two daughters from going to school and sent them to work in some houses. Finally, all the four members of the family went to work for a very meagre salary to run their life. The son of the family alone continued his education. Ramu's boss was a very kind hearted person. Every day he noticed the hard work of Ramu. At present, Ramu was working in the farm house of his boss. The boss also had a departmental store of his own. The boss appointed Ramu in his departmental store as the supervisor because of his hard work and honest behavior. Ramu's life began to shine. He began to settle in a very well manner. He renovated his hut in to a cement building. He settled his two daughter's life by getting them married to a good person. They lived good and well with their family. Ramu's son completed his education and got a good job. Ramu was happy and satisfied with the life and progress of his children. All this happened due to the persistence and the way he labored hard.

SWEAT, DETERMINATION & HARD WORK MAKES LIFE A MAGIC.

CHAPTER SIXTEEN

FARMING

M. MADHUBALA,CLASS 9, Sri KGS HSS, Aduthurai

Vellanppavai was a beautiful village. There lived a poor farmer named Ravi with his wife Meenatchi and their only daughter Karkuzhali. Ravi's family background was very poor. His parents were uneducated and he had no inherited properties. The family ran only with Ravi's earnings. He had a small plot of land and worked hard in it with wife's continuous support. Karkuzhali was a soft natured, kind-hearted, talented girl studying in class 12. She got first mark in district level in her public examination. The whole village appreciated her. She craved to study B. Sc in Agriculture. She knew about the difficulties the farmers faced in farming. She wished to save agriculture as she knew very well that no one get good food without farmers and farming. Though Ravi was very poor, he encouraged his daughter to study. Although his financial condition was very worst, he managed to make arrangements for her studies. Karkuzhali wrote well in the entrance exam and got admission in an agriculture college in Chennai.

Ravi and Meenatchi worked hard in their paddy fields. Unfortunately, due to heavy rain, there was a great loss for them. They suffered even for their basic needs. But they never informed anything about this to Karkuzhali. On the other hand, Karkuzhali faced many issues in her college because of her classmates. They teased and humiliated her as she was from a village. Semester exams started. She wrote four exams very well. A serious problem turned out for her before the last exam because of her classmates Priyanka and Rohith. They both were jealous of Karkuzhali because once the teachers who were friendly with them began to support and motivate Karkuzhali now. They revenged against Karkuzhali. They hid bit papers in her place and complained to the principal. Without any queries, the principal didn't allow her to write the exam. After examination, Priyanka and Rohith happily teased her and admitted that they were the reason for everything. Accidentally the principal heard everything and suspended them. Then Karkuzhali completed her graduation successfully. She taught everyone in her village to farm in their lands without any chemical manures. Vellanppavai became very famous in natural farming. Karkuzhali became the heroine of the village.

FARMING ISN'T JUST A JOB, IT'S THE WAY OF LIFE.

CHAPTER SEVENTEEN

CHILDHOOD MEMORIES

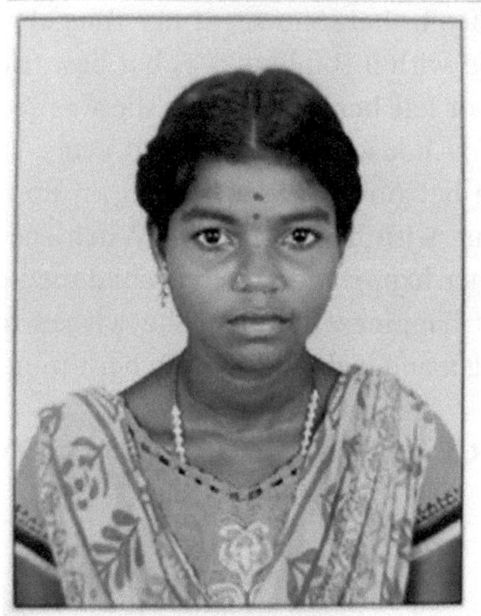

P. MADHUSRI,CLASS 9, Sri KGS HSS, Aduthurai.

Madhu was a little girl of 15. Even now she remembered what had happened in her third birthday. Her parents presented her a toy house which was really big like a tent. She thought it as one of her most valuable gifts in her life. The house was so simple and beautiful with different colors. The roof was blue in color, the windows were brown in color and the other things were in white color completely. It was such a colorful and wonderful gift. She always tried a lot to decorate the toy house with different things. The size of the house was same as her height at that time. She liked the house very much because of its size. The size fitted her perfectly to sit inside the house. Many times she slept inside the toy house. She loved her toy house that much. Her happiness knew no bounds when she was with it. The house also had a music system which attracted her more towards it as she was a music lover. The house was made of wood, the windows were of glasses and the roof was of plastic. The designs in the roof and windows looked like hand made that is so cute. All these fascinated her and had a powerful influence in her. She spent her time always with it. She talked and played with it thinking it as her best friend but it never hurts her or never left her alone when she was sad. It entertained her a lot. Her toy house knew each and every stage of her life. She used to hug her house. Even as a grown up now, she always like to spent time with her toy house. When she saw the house, it remembered her happy and precious childhood days. The house was a source of happiness for her. She wished to keep it safely without breaking it and it should be with her throughout her life till her last breath.

MEMORIES OF CHILDHOOD LASTS LONGER AND STRONGER.

CHAPTER EIGHTEEN

KINDNESS

M. MAHALAKSHMI,CLASS 9, Sri KGS HSS, Aduthurai

John was a selfish boy. He never shared his toys or anything else with anyone. His parents were worried very much about teaching him kindness and sharing. One day John was returning home from school in his new bicycle. On the way he saw a boy falling into the drainage and getting hurt himself. The boy cried for help and moaned in pain. John was not that kind of personality who is ready to help others. But that day when he witnessed the boy suffering with pain, he felt sad for the boy. So, he rushed to help the boy. He lent his hand to the boy and lifted him. He told the boy that it looked like that his hand was fractured. He took the boy to the hospital in his bicycle. The doctors treated the boy good and well. Later John informed the boy's parents about the incident. John had waited in the hospital till the boy's parents came. The boy's parents came and thanked John for his timely help. After few days the boy's parents visited John and thanked him again. They said that John was a very kind person and also blessed him that god will be always with him. When they left the house, John's father was amazed by his son's behavior. He also felt very happy when he came to know that John had understand the importance of being kind. He also advised John to be kind always.

KINDNESS IS THE KEY TO OPEN THE HEARTS OF OTHERS.

CHAPTER NINETEEN

THE MAGICAL BOOK

S. MOHANASRI
CLASS 9

As I flipped the pages of the dusty old book, I noticed that many pages were missing. I found the book in my attic. It looked mysterious and caught my attention immediately. It was very rustic and the pages were crinkly. The name of the book was "The Mysterious Night of Armageddon". The room was so quiet. My parents went to pick up my sister from her hostel. I held the book firmly and as I flipped the book, it started glowing in a magical way. I had never seen a book glow without a phone inside it. Soon I felt asleep. My body felt weak as I was sucked inside the book. Immediately I woke up and thought it was surely a dream. I told myself that I was still in the attic. I got down from the attic and walked towards the kitchen as I was really too hungry. My mother was preparing food in the kitchen. I was shocked to see my sister. She came from her hostel as a two days holiday to home. I approached my mother slowly with the tip of my feet. She turned around and at once I was frightened to see her. She had horns, huge body and large burning red eyes with terrible looking teeth. I ran back to the attic fast and closed the door. I saw my mother running behind me. I fell on my knees and started crying. The door started rumbling with loud noise. I was very scared of my own mother. The knock of the door grew louder and my hands started trembling in fear. I held the book again and prayed to go back from where I was but nothing happened. I was totally broken. I started sweating badly. The knocks of the door grew louder and louder. I fell on the ground and started weeping. After sometime I fell asleep for a longtime. When I woke up, I was in my bed and my mother was standing there scolding me that I was too late. I thought myself that what had happened and I came to the conclusion that everything was just a dream.

BOOKS ARE UNIQUE PORTABLE MAGIC.

CHAPTER TWENTY

PERSEVERANCE

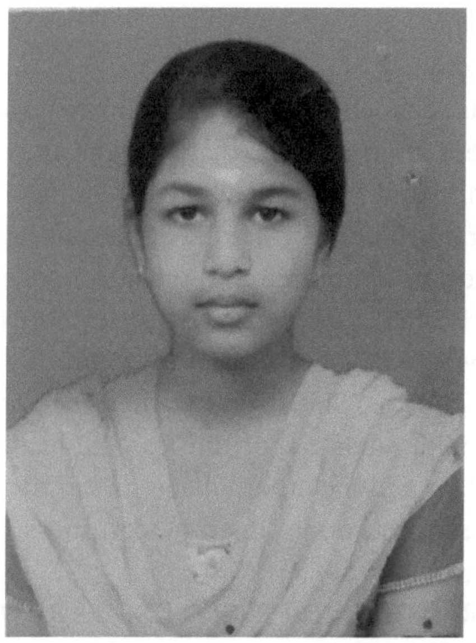

K. PRIYADHARSHINI,CLASS 9, Sri KGS HSS, Aduthurai.

Once there lived a poor girl in a village. Her name was Rasi. She was fifteen years old. She lived with her mother and her elder sister. Her father was no more. He expired when Raji was three years old. Raji was a good-natured girl. She always wished for the goodness and improvement of her village. She determined to become an IAS officer. She strongly craved to become the district collector in her own district and wanted to develop her own village by all means. She wanted her villagers to be benefitted by the government. She studied eagerly with full concentration. She prepared well for her higher secondary exam. Though she scored first mark in district, she just joined an undergraduate degree. Then she started going for coaching classes to achieve her dream of becoming an IAS officer. Her sister supported and encouraged her a lot. Raji always kept in mind and remembered our former president Dr. A.P.J. Abdul Kalam's words

"I am the best, I can do it,
God is always with me
I am the winner
Today is my day"

These words echoed in her ears always and inspired her completely. These are the words that acted as an energizer for her. Her perseverance and persistence gave her the fruit of success. She became a rank holder in her UPSC exams. After completing her training, she was appointed as the district collector in her own district as she wished. She resolved to develop her village. She motivated the women of her village to dream big and work hard to achieve their dreams. She always wanted men and women to be treated equally with equal opportunities. She made a resolution to improve her village and the other villages in her district. She wished to make her district a model district for others. She wished her country to shine in all ways.

PERSEVERANCE AND PERSISTENCE ARE OMNIPOTENT

CHAPTER TWENTY-ONE

MOTHER'S LOVE

S. SAVITHA,CLASS 9, Sri KGS HSS, Aduthurai.

Raja and his mother Devi lived in a small town. Raja's father died when he was a child. So, he spent his life only with his mother. But Raja hated her mother very much. He didn't understand the true love and affection of his mother. He always used to scold her for his life with lack of money and luxurious facilities. He felt downtrodden as her mother was working in a restaurant and washing the plates that everyone ate. Though Raja disliked his mother a lot and shouted at her always, she remained calm with a smiling face all the time. She thought of satisfying her son with what he needs. To prove her love and care for her son, one day she asked Raja with what he would be happy. She said that she would do whatever he wanted. Raja asked for a bike. Few days later, after a great struggle Devi managed to gift a bike to Raja. Raja felt so happy and excited on seeing the bike. His happiness knew no bounds without the knowledge of her mother's struggle and pain in proving her affection towards his son. Raja always roamed in the bike. He met his friends and went for a long drive with them. On the way back to home, they met with an accident. Raja was very badly injured and he was in a very serious condition. Doctors couldn't say whether he would survive or not and also said that he had to undergo a heart transplant surgery immediately. After the surgery, Raja was getting alright little by little. His friend was with him. Raja asked his friend about his mother. He reluctantly said that his mother was no more. Raja was shocked to hear the news. His friend said what had happened after his accident. He told that when Raja's mother heard about the accident, she got a severe heart attack. Though we tried our best to save her, all our efforts failed and she died. Her heart was implanted to you. She saved you and your life even after her death. When Raja heard all this, he started crying. He wept and realized his mistake. Now he had totally changed and understood her mother and her flawless love in her absence.

MOTHER'S LOVE – THE PUREST FORM OF LOVE.

CHAPTER TWENTY-TWO

THE LITTLE GIRL'S CONFIDENCE

R. SINDHUJA,CLASS 9, Sri KGS HSS, Aduthurai.

There lived a little girl in a small town. Her name was Kayalvizhi. She lived with his parents, grandparents and brothers. Her father's name was Siva and he was an excellent tailor. Her mother Suseela was a housewife. Her grandfather was a farmer. Her grandmother was a retired teacher. She had an elder brother Raghu who was doing his graduation. He was a good sportsman too. Her younger brother Ravi was a school going student. Raghu and Ravi were intelligent and both shone well in whatever they did. But Kayalvizhi was not very smart. Though she was interested in learning new things, she couldn't cope up with everything. Her brothers teased her. Everyone around her scolded and criticized her for not studying well. All their words demotivated Kayalvizhi. But Kayalvizhi's father and grandmother supported her a lot. They encouraged that she would achieve in her life surely and also assured that she would become a great person. She started studying well. Though she worked hard, she scored only average marks. She didn't give up hope. Her father sent her for special tuition classes. He motivated Kayalvizhi by saying," Try, try and keep on trying, till you succeed." Kayalvizhi kept her father's words in her mind. It was always ringing in her ears. Keeping her father's words in mind, she studied well. She succeeded in her attempt. Her hope, confidence and hard work gave her the fruit of success. Everyone those who scolded her, now appreciated her for her achievement.

CONFIDENCE – THE MOST BEAUTIFUL ORNAMENT TO WEAR.

CHAPTER TWENTY-THREE

HUMANITY

R. SNEKHA,CLASS 9, Sri KGS HSS, Aduthurai.

There was a man named Ram in a town. He thought that he was the only sincere hard worker and nothing would happen without him. He never spent time with his family. One day on his way back to home from his office, he met with an accident and died. After death, he stood in a place where the path bifurcated, one to the heaven and the other to the hell. God appeared in front of Ram and asked him where he would like to go. Ram replied that he wished to go to the heaven. God asked the reason why he wished to go the heaven. Ram said that he was so perfect in everything. Nothing would happen perfectly in his office and also at his home without him. So, he was completely eligible to enter into the heaven. God continued to say that he would give him a second chance for his soul to visit the earth for ten days to perceive the beauty of the earth and to understand what the real life is. Ram's soul visited the earth and saw the heavenly beauty of the earth where it lived. Then it visited the work place and understood that even in his absence everything went well. No one cares about his absence too. Then the soul liked to see the family. All the members of the family were so sad because of his absence. Ram's soul comprehended that family was a hidden treasure on earth. Finally, the soul came back to God and informed that he had wasted his life without knowing any values of the human life. He also added that he would like to apologize to his company security guard for suspecting him without any evidence for a theft without giving him any chance to explain his side. He also dismissed the security guard without any enquiry charging against him as a thief. On hearing all these, God replied that he didn't want to feel for that as the security got a good job after that incident. His family was settled well. The security was thanking Ram every day for that. Informing all this, God took Ram to the heaven as he really felt sorry his mistakes.

HUMANITY CAN'T SURVIVE WITHOUT LOVE, COMPASSION AND UNDERSTANDING.

CHAPTER TWENTY-FOUR

WORLD IS A MIRROR

S. SOWMIYADEVI,CLASS 9, Sri KGS HSS, Aduthurai.

Once there was a museum in a small town. In the museum, there was a small room which was made of mirrors completely. It had a wall, roof and even the floor was made of mirrors. One day, a caretaker of the museum forgot to lock the back door of the museum that led directly to the room made of mirror. A dog was roaming near the museum and by mistake it entered the mirror room. When the dog was in the middle of the room, it saw the reflection of its own image on the mirror. It thought that it was surrounded by a whole pack of dogs from all sides. Seeing that, the dog got scared and started barking at the mirror images. The dog noticed that all the dogs were barking at him in the same way. The echoes after hitting at the mirrors, got magnified. Frightened by the sound, the dog started to bark frantically. Next morning, when the caretaker entered the room, he found the lifeless body of the dog. There was no one to harm the dog yet it died fighting at its own reflection without knowing the truth. Everything around us is the reflection of our own thoughts, feelings and actions. The world is like a mirror. Whatever you show it reflects. Know your strength and try to be positive always and do good to others.

THE WORLD IS A GREAT MIRROR THAT REFLECTS BACK WHAT YOU ARE.

CHAPTER TWENTY-FIVE

POWER OF NATURE

S. SOUNDHARYA,CLASS 9, Sri KGS HSS, Aduthurai.

A little boy named Raju lived in a city with his parents and grandparents. Raju liked and loved his grandparents very much. His grandmother used to tell him a story every day before he slept. Similarly, one day also Raju asked his grandmother for a story. She wondered what type of story to tell him. Suddenly there was a power cut. Immediately grandma lit a candle. Still Raju was waiting for the story. Grandma decided to tell him about her childhood village life during olden days. She told that when she was a child, she lived with her parents in a small cottage. There was no electricity. We used to light our house by lighting lamps of clay. Her parents were hard working farmers. Raju asked her curiously to tell about her village. Grandma said that her village was a very beautiful place seemed like a heaven on earth surrounded by many water bodies such as ponds, rivers, lakes etc. with green fields on both sides of the road. They didn't have water taps or water tanks for water. They walked some distance to fetch good water for drinking and cooking from a well. There were no gas stoves or kerosene stoves even to cook. They cooked in stoves and vessels which was made of clay. Though they didn't have any modern technology or hi-tech facilities, everything they had, seemed healthy and happy. She also added that her village also had a wide variety of plants, trees, herbs, shrubs and vines. Raju asked innocently why those beautiful scenery of nature was missing nowadays. Grandma said that we had destroyed the beauty of nature because of our greediness to build houses and to set up factories. We cut trees mindlessly to get papers and also for construction. Because of all these, we are suffering now. The trees once cut by us wasn't replaced properly. So, there's a deficit in rainfall that leads to water scarcity. Due to lack of trees, we're facing many environmental problems too. Raju fell asleep after listening to all told by his grandmother. The next morning, Raju woke up as a new person. He took a vow to plant more plants and trees to save nature.

SAVE TREES, SAVE NATURE.

CHAPTER TWENTY-SIX

REAL TREASURE

R. SURIYAKALA,CLASS 9, Sri KGS HSS, Aduthurai.

Vishnu was a happy man living in a city. He led his life happily with his mother Anjali, wife Jaanu and his children Priya and Ram. Vishnu lived in a rental house. His dream was to build a new house with all amenities. He was working in a company as a supervisor. Once the company offered Vishnu a great opportunity. The company gave him promotion and informed him to move to one of its branches in a foreign country as a contract for three years. The salary was also doubled. Vishnu readily accepted the offer as he knew that it would help him in fulfilling his dream. But his family insisted him not to go. His wife was too worried whether she would manage the family without Vishnu. But Vishnu never gave his ears to all those words. He got ready and left abroad. He worked hard with dedication. Three years rolled on easily. Vishnu earned a lot. He had enough money to build his dream house. But Vishnu was not satisfied. He extended his work visa for three more years. He continued his job with full involvement. One day while at work, he fell down from the stairs in his office. He was injured badly and his right leg was fractured. He was admitted in the hospital. He had more money but there was no one to take care of him. He felt very lonely. He thought again and again about his family. He thought about the love and care of his family. He felt that he was missing something in his life. Suddenly he received a bad news from his native that his mother had expired. He was not able to go even to do the final funeral rites for his mother. Now he realized that a lovable family was the real treasure in life and without the family there was no use of being wealthy. Immediately he decided to resign his job. He resigned his job and reached his native to meet his family. He started a business of his own. He started living a meaningful life. He lived very happily with his family. He never forgot the lesson which life had taught him.

LOVABLE FAMILY IS THE REAL TREASURE WORTH MORE THAN A MOUNTAIN OF GOLD.

CHAPTER TWENTY-SEVEN

THE MAGICAL TOY

G. THIRUPPAVAI,CLASS 9, Sri KGS HSS, Aduthurai.

A poor family lived in a small village. The family had Krishna, the father, Shanthi, the mother and their only son Sam. Krishna was a hardworking labour. Shanthi was a home maker. Sam was an angry bird. He was so mischievous too.

Always he did lot of pranks. Because of these behaviors, no one liked Sam. Everyone in the village scolded him for his non-stop pranks. In school also, there was no friends for Sam. No one played with him even didn't speak a word with him because of his anger. There is no one to support him. No one spoke in favor of Sam if any problem arises. On seeing all these, Krishna was worried so much. He wished that his son would study well. He also thought that his son wouldn't suffer as a labor like them. He wanted his son to be settled in a high position with a good job. Shanthi too worried when she witnessed the village people cursing her son. She had a strong desire to see a lot of changes in her son from his bad attitudes.

One day Sam went to the playground. He saw the boys playing there. He asked if he could also join them but they didn't allow him. So, he sat on a pile of sand and started digging it. After sometime, he found a toy carved out of stone. It looked so cute and beautiful. Actually, it was a magical toy. It reflected whatever Sam had done. Slowly it became Sam's best friend. If Sam was happy, the toy too was happy. If Sam was angry, it too reacted angrily. But Sam didn't like the angry face of the toy. So, he stopped behaving angrily and realized the reason why everyone hated him. There was a drastic change in him. He completely stopped his pranks. He was so kind to everyone and started helping everyone. He also started to study well. One day the toy was broken. Even after that Sam didn't change his attitude. He got first mark in his exams. The people of the village who cursed him once applauded him now for his achievement in studies and also for his kind behaviour.

TRUE LOVE AND KINDNESS CHANGES EVERYTHING.

CHAPTER TWENTY-EIGHT

LOVE FOR FARMERS

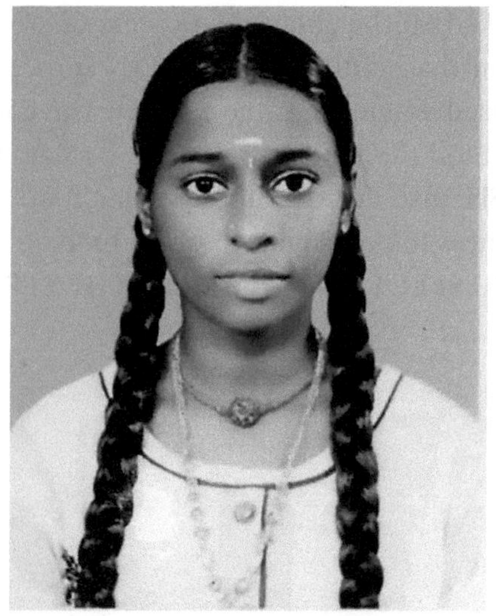

S. UDHAYA,CLASS 9, Sri KGS HSS, Aduthurai.

Indu was a girl of dazzling beauty. She lived in a city. She always wished to roam around the world. Though she lived in a city, she liked villages very much. As she was in her summer vacation, she craved to visit her native village. Her father arranged for her trip. Indu reached her village happily. A man named Muthu received her. Muthu was a man of simplicity. That village is his native. He loved his village very much. He was the caretaker of Indu whenever she came to the village. Indu was excited so much when she reached the village. She ran as a deer in the grass lawn. She jumped in the river water and played in the water like a beautiful swan. Muthu followed her shouting to go slowly. She enjoyed the beauty of nature. She told Muthu that she loved the place as it was so calm and peaceful. She also told Muthu that she felt thirsty. Immediately Muthu got her a tender coconut. She relished it and she loved it because of its taste. After sometimes, they crossed beautiful paddy fields on both sides of the road. Indu wished to walk in that field. Muthu said that we should not walk in that. He also said that if she like, she can touch the soil and the crops. Indu touched as if touching a feather. She felt so elated and asked Muthu about the process of growing paddy and getting rice from that. Muthu explained the process step by step. Indu was surprised when she came to knew the complete process. She also understood the hard work of the farmers behind the rice we are eating. She also decided not to waste food anymore and to create an awareness to people not to waste food.

GIVE RESPECT TO FARMERS – THE LIVING GOD

CHAPTER TWENTY-NINE

AN AMBITIOUS GIRL

S. VAISHNAVI,CLASS 9, Sri KGS HSS, Aduthurai.

Once upon a time, there lived a poor girl in a village. She was a hard worker by nature. One day she went to the village market to sell milk. She collected milk from various houses and sold it in the market to lead her life. The pot which she was carrying on her head was full of milk. On her way to the market, she began to make plans to use her money when she earns a lot through her business. At first, she thought of buying some chicks. By getting more eggs from the grown chicks, she thought of getting more chicks to develop her business. Then she planned to sell all the hens for a good lump sum amount. With the money she earned from the hens, she thought of getting some goats and cows. Further, she would sell the grownup goats for a good value and will buy more cows. Then she will start the milk business from her own investment. She will shine as a successful business woman. She will build a beautiful house with the money earned. She will buy expensive jewelry and beautiful clothes. She will look so cute and beautiful as a princess. She felt so happy when she was thinking of all these happenings about the progress in her life. To make her dreams come true, as the first step of reaching her ambition, she started working hard. She was determined to reach her goal as an ambitious girl.

EVERYTHING PROSPERS WITH HARDWORK.

CHAPTER THIRTY

NEVER EVER GIVE UP

S. VISHALINI,CLASS 9, Sri KGS HSS, Aduthurai

Long time ago, there lived a man in a village. He lived happily with his family. He had his own land and he did farming in it whole heartedly. He worked hard with dedication. He loved his fields very much. But his happiness couldn't last long as the village faced a severe drought. He and the other villagers struggled and suffered a lot. They desperately waited for rain but they were unlucky. There was no rain. Regrettably all the lands, crops and even trees dried up. The cattle and cows started dying. As there was no rain, the wells, streams, ponds and rivers too dried up slowly.

One night, during a meet of the villagers, the man said," Friends, we all had a very hard time. We had heard tales from our elders about the perennial river running under the earth through our village. Why didn't we dig and try to find the river for water?". The villagers agreed and everyone started digging. They dug for some days continuously but gave up soon as they didn't get anything. However, the man who told about the river, without giving up hope and confidence kept on digging continuously. When the village people insisted him to stop digging, he refused strongly and kept on working tirelessly. After several days of his hard work, one fine morning he found the river with tasty water when he had dug deep enough. His attitude of not giving up saved the entire village. He became the role model for the youngsters of the village. The man advised the villagers not to give up easily in anything. Now they never met with shortage of water. Everyone in the village continued farming happily. The villagers also understood, "Where there is a problem, there is a solution always." They all came up together and found a solution whatever crises they faced. This confidence came to them because of the man.

NEVER EVER GIVE UP, KEEP YOURSELF ENCOURAGED.

About The Author

Mrs. S. SUMATHI., M.A., B.Ed.,EDITOR AND PUBLISHER

Mrs.S.Sumathi, has the degree of M.A(English) & B.Ed. She has been working in Sri KGS HSS, Aduthurai, Thiruvidaimarudur TK, Thanjavur Dt, a Govt aided school. Her goal is to get Dr.Radhakrishnan's "The Best Teacher" Award. She is a budding short story Writer. One of her short stories was published in "Sparkles of Short Stories" and "Spitfire Soul." She has written more than 500 poems on various topics. Her first 100 string of poems were published by December 2020 in the name of "String of Pearls." Her second book of 100 poems "Drizzling of Verses" was published by October 2021. She has published a book of 180 quotes **"REPLICA"** recently. Apart from this, she has been a co-author in "Rainbow of Verses", "Mesmerizing Honey Drops", "Profound Writers Anthology", "Echoes" "Glitters of Creative Writers" and

"Forbidden clouds." One of her poems was published in "The beauty of creation and love", a World Book of Records in which 1111 poems were there written by 1111 poets. Her articles and poems were published in Namaste India, an E-magazine. One of her poems was published in Kenya Times daily newspaper. She is a receiver of “Kalvi Ratna Award”,”Arivu Sudar Gandhi Award”, ”Kalam Arivu Maamani Award”, “Best Teacher 2020 Award”, “Woman of Excellence Award”, “FCP Excellence Award”, “All India Best Writer (AIBA) Award” "Kalvi Sindanaiyalar Award" Paavendharin "Semmozhi thendral award" and certified as one of the “Best Writers”, one of the “Consistent Writers” in the Profound Writers group. Always she wishes to be the best teacher and the best human.

9 798887 047331

Printed by Libri Plureos GmbH in Hamburg, Germany